save the . . .
GORILLAS

by **Anita Sanchez**
with an introduction
by **Chelsea Clinton**

PHILOMEL

This is for Aimee

PHILOMEL BOOKS
An imprint of Penguin Random House LLC, New York

First published in the United States of America by Philomel Books,
an imprint of Penguin Random House LLC, 2023

Text copyright © 2023 by Chelsea Clinton

Photo credits: page 2: © okyela/Adobe Stock; page 4: © Morphart/Adobe Stock; page 5:
© rjcoulstock/Adobe Stock; pages 9 and 33: © Wikimedia Commons; pages 18 and 57:
© Bob Campbell Papers, African Studies Collections, Special and Area Studies Collections,
George A. Smathers Libraries, University of Florida, Gainesville, FL.; page 20: Lmspencer/
Adobe Stock; pages 22 and 53: © Marian/Adobe Stock; page 25: © paula/Adobe Stock;
page 39: © Wirestock Creators/Adobe Stock; page 44: © Anita Sanchez; page 67: © asaf/
Adobe Stock

Visit us online at penguinrandomhouse.com.

Library of Congress Cataloging-in-Publication Data is available.

Printed in the United States of America

ISBN 9780593404089 (hardcover)
ISBN 9780593404096 (paperback)

1st Printing

LSCC

Edited by Talia Benamy and Jill Santopolo
Design by Lily Qian
Text set.in Calisto MT Pro

save the . . .

save the . . .
BLUE WHALES

save the . . .
ELEPHANTS

save the . . .
FROGS

save the . . .
GIRAFFES

save the . . .
GORILLAS

save the . . .
LIONS

save the . . .
POLAR BEARS

save the . . .
TIGERS

save the . . .
WHALE SHARKS

Dear Reader,

When I was around your age, my favorite animals were dinosaurs and elephants. I wanted to know everything I could about triceratopses, stegosauruses and other dinosaurs that had roamed our earth millions of years ago. Elephants, though, captured my curiosity and my heart. The more I learned about the largest animals on land today, the more I wanted to do to help keep them and other endangered species safe forever.

So I joined organizations working around the world to support endangered species and went to our local zoo to learn more about conservation efforts close to home (thanks to my parents and grandparents). I tried to learn as much as I could about how we can ensure animals and plants don't go extinct like the dinosaurs, especially since it's the choices that we're making that pose the greatest threat to their lives today.

The choices we make don't have to be huge to make

a real difference. When I was in elementary school, I used to cut up the plastic rings around six-packs of soda, glue them to brightly colored construction paper (purple was my favorite) and hand them out to whomever would take one in a one-girl campaign to raise awareness about the dangers that plastic six-pack rings posed to marine wildlife around the world. I learned about that from a book—*50 Simple Things Kids Can Do to Save the Earth*—which helped me understand that you're never too young to make a difference and that we all can change the world. I hope that this book will inform and inspire you to help save this and other endangered species. There are tens of thousands of species that are currently under threat, with more added every year. We have the power to save those species, and with your help, we can.

Sincerely,

Chelsea Clinton

save the . . .
GORILLAS

CONTENTS

-- -- -- -- -- -- -- -- -- -- -- -- -- -

1

OUR COUSINS IN THE RAINFOREST

What happens if you tickle a gorilla? And would you dare to try?

Gorillas are big animals that can be really, really scary. They have huge fangs, enormous muscles, and can weigh over four hundred pounds. Sometimes a male gorilla will pound his chest and let out a terrifying roar. Their massive arms are strong enough to tear down trees and bend iron bars. Who wouldn't be scared?

But it turns out that gorillas aren't as

A fierce roar—or a lazy yawn?

dangerous as they look. They don't eat people—
in fact, for the most part, they don't eat meat
at all, just plants. Gorillas can be gentle friends
and tender, loving parents. And they really like
to laugh.

Scientists used to think that humans were the only species that could laugh. But research has shown that other kinds of animals can laugh, too. Gorillas make sounds that are very similar to the sounds people make when they're having fun. They snort, giggle, and chuckle when they're tickled by playmates or when one of their brothers or sisters is chasing them playfully.

Humans and gorillas may look different on the outside—after all, gorillas are covered with fur, while we have thick hair on only a few places on our bodies. But underneath all that fur, gorillas are more like humans than you might first think.

Humans and gorillas are both primates, a group of mammals that includes monkeys, apes, and lemurs. Gorillas are some of our

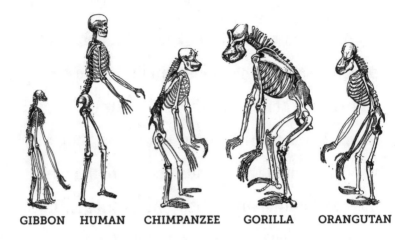

GIBBON   HUMAN   CHIMPANZEE   GORILLA   ORANGUTAN

Under the skin, we're a lot like gorillas.

closest relatives. Both people and gorillas have five digits (fingers or toes) on each arm and leg. We both have eyes that look straight ahead. Adult humans have the same number of teeth as adult gorillas: thirty-two. And unlike most mammals, neither humans nor gorillas have tails. Gorilla bones, hearts, livers, and kidneys all look a lot like ours—just bigger.

But of course, there are a lot of ways we're different from gorillas, too. One difference is in numbers. There are more than 7,000,000,000 human beings on the planet. There are only about 100,000 gorillas.

Another big difference is our habitat. Human beings live all over the planet, in every kind of place you can imagine: tropical islands, frozen tundra, dry deserts, and swampy wetlands.

Gorillas have fingers and opposable thumbs, just like us.

Gorillas live only in Central Africa, in a region near the equator called the Congo Basin. And they live only in one kind of place: the misty, moist, green habitat called a rainforest.

A Forest for Gorillas

Rainforests are ancient environments. They existed on our planet millions of years ago, and in some places, they really haven't changed much over time. Rainforests have closely packed trees forming a leafy roof that blocks the sun and keeps the ground damp and shady. Tall trees are draped with vines and flowering orchids, while grasses and shrubs grow underneath. The Congo rainforest has more than 10,000 different kinds of plants! Since gorillas are plant-eaters, the rainforest is like a giant supermarket filled with the foods they need.

The rainforest stretches through many countries, including Cameroon, Gabon, Central African Republic, Democratic Republic of the Congo (DRC), Republic of the Congo, Equatorial Guinea, Rwanda, Uganda, and Nigeria. It's home to countless different kinds of living things: birds, bats, butterflies, fungi, fish, ferns, and more. There are hundreds of species of mammals, including chimpanzees, forest elephants, hippos, and leopards. And it's the only place in the world where gorillas live wild and free.

Not all parts of this giant forest are the same. If you visited the swampy lowlands of Gabon, you'd be hot and sweaty—but if you climbed up the steep mountains in Rwanda, you might shiver with cold. These mountains are so high that the temperatures are often chilly, and damp mists drift through the trees.

Scientists have identified two different species of gorillas, which don't interbreed: Eastern gorillas and Western gorillas. These two species live about five hundred miles apart, on opposite sides of the Congo River. Both Eastern and Western gorillas have two subspecies. (A subspecies is a group that doesn't interbreed with any other group in the wild, although it possibly could, if they were brought together in a zoo.)

Western gorillas live in hot, humid lowland areas, where the temperature rarely gets below 70°F. They have by far the biggest population, although most of them live in remote areas so it's hard to know for sure how many there are. There might be close to 100,000. A subspecies of Western gorillas called Cross

Can you tell these two species apart?
Western gorilla (left), Eastern gorilla (right).

River gorillas was once thought to be extinct. But in the 1980s, scientists discovered a tiny population hidden in a small area of highland forest on the border of Cameroon and Nigeria. No one is sure how many there are—there might be as few as 250.

The biggest gorillas in the world are Eastern

lowland gorillas (sometimes they're called Grauer's gorillas). The males can reach 450 pounds and stand six foot five. Scientists estimate that their numbers have shrunk a lot in recent years. Most of these huge animals are clustered in one small region of the DRC. But this is an area that has been torn by civil war and is often patrolled by armed soldiers. It's a very dangerous place for wildlife researchers, and so it's hard to get an exact count of wildlife. There are now approximately 8,000 of these big animals.

The other subspecies of Eastern gorilla is the mountain gorilla. Approximately 1,000 of these shaggy animals remain, mostly in national parks in Rwanda and Uganda. Mountain gorillas have much thicker fur than gorillas that live in hotter parts of the rainforest.

Gorilla Gardeners

Like a lot of people, gorillas love to eat! Just like us, a gorilla will sometimes go "mmmmmm" when savoring something really tasty. Many gorillas have a sweet tooth, and they love sticky, sugary fruit. And it turns out that's a really good thing, because their fruit habit is the rainforest's future. Gorillas are helping to plant forests with every bite they take.

How does a gorilla plant a tree? Well, many rainforest plants have hard seeds inside the delicious fruity part. As a gorilla gobbles down a fruit, it swallows the seeds inside whole. For most of the day, the gorilla eats—and then at night, the gorilla makes a nest for sleeping, grabbing branches and tucking them into a round pile that looks like a giant bird's nest. And after a good night's sleep, the gorilla is likely to do what a lot of people do first thing in the morning: They poop! Gorillas often poop in their nests (which doesn't matter, because they build a new one in a different place every night).

The gorilla's droppings are filled with seeds from the fruits the animal has eaten. So the seeds are deposited in an open area where the gorillas have pulled down some branches for nest-building. That means those areas will get sunshine and rain. The seeds are surrounded by gorilla poop, which is moist and filled with nutrients. Sun, water, and fertilizer—just what seeds need to sprout!

Many of the seeds planted by gorillas will grow into new trees. And since gorillas constantly roam the rainforest, they spread seeds far and wide. Other animals like birds or mice also spread small seeds, but not the large pits found inside many rainforest fruits. Gorillas are big animals, so they can swallow big seeds, ones too large to pass through the stomachs of most animals.

Gorillas play a major role in creating the diversity of the rainforest. Without gorillas, this habitat would be a very different place, lacking most of the fruit trees that animals need for food. Fruit bats, monkeys, parrots, elephants, forest hogs, antelope, butterflies: so many creatures depend on the gorilla gardeners.

2

FAMILIES IN THE FOREST

Have you ever heard of King Kong? He's a giant gorilla in a blockbuster movie who knocks over houses, stomps on cars, and even climbs the Empire State Building to battle airplanes— and needless to say, he never existed in real life! The first King Kong movie was made in 1933. Back then, almost nothing was known about gorillas. A few hunters had contributed gorilla skins or bones to museums, and there were a few gorillas caged in circuses and zoos, but only a couple of brief attempts had been made to study gorillas in the wild. All that was known for sure was that gorillas would roar and beat their chests, baring their fangs in fury when a human approached.

In 1957, a young zoology student decided to get to know these mysterious creatures. George Schaller traveled to the rainforest of the Congo to study mountain gorillas. Led by guides from the Ba'Aka community who had lived in the rainforest for generations, George clambered up the steep slopes of the Virunga Mountains. He saw gorilla tracks and droppings and passed places where they had splintered branches and chewed on leaves. Finally, he spotted a group of dark shapes clustered among the dense forest growth. Nervously, he tiptoed toward his first gorillas.

George watched the peaceful group as they sat munching on plants. He noticed how the gorillas' fur shone a deep blue-black against the intense green of the rainforest leaves. Gorilla youngsters played a rowdy game of tag around a wrinkled elder fast asleep in the sun. He saw a mother tenderly nurse her baby, then held his breath as a huge male came over and reached out a massive paw toward the helpless infant. But the father tenderly cradled the baby, stroking it gently.

Over the course of several months, George found that he could recognize individual gorillas by the shapes of their eyes and noses and the expressions on their faces, just as you recognize your family members. The gorillas didn't seem to mind him hanging around, and he hoped to move closer to them so he could spend time studying their behavior. But his research was suddenly interrupted by a disaster that's terrible for gorillas and humans alike: war. In 1960, a brutal civil war broke out in the Congo and all wildlife research was halted.

Woman in the Mist

As the war raged on, George moved to other remote places to study different species of wildlife, but a few years later, another brave researcher went to the rainforest to carry on his work. Dian Fossey was an American primatologist, which is someone who studies animals like gorillas, chimpanzees, and more. She spent much of her life in the misty upland rainforest and came to love the mountain gorillas as though they were her own family.

Dian spent months getting the gorillas to

Dian Fossey lived with gorillas in their beautiful, remote mountain habitat.

accept her so that they would go about their normal behavior in her presence. She discovered that the way to win their trust was to act like a gorilla herself. She would scratch herself, roll on her back, or squat as the gorillas did. She learned to knuckle-walk, bent over and swinging herself along on her fists. She would pretend to munch wild celery. Dian soon learned not to make eye contact with her new friends, as a direct stare seems like a threat to a gorilla, and they would move away from her nervously. Finally, one day a gorilla reached out and touched her hand.

To help tell the gorillas apart, she gave them names, like Peanuts, Puck, and Effie. Her favorite was a young male she named Digit because he had an oddly shaped finger that must have been broken at some point. When she first met him, he was only about five years old, "a bright-eyed, inquisitive ball of fluff." He was curious and friendly, rolling over and kicking his legs in the air as if to invite her to play. Soon she could romp and wrestle with him. Digit would sit next to her, share food, and sometimes put his arm around her shoulders in a friendly hug.

One day she watched Digit as he jumped

onto the lap of a big male she called Uncle Bert. The adult gorilla picked a handful of flowers and used them to tickle the youngster, which brought "loud play chuckles and a big toothy grin from Digit."

As she sat among the gorillas, Dian recorded their movements, their habits, and the way they behaved toward each other. She kept careful

Baby gorillas love to play!

notes on every detail of their lives from morning till night, jotting down what she observed in her notebook—although she had to look out for playful young gorillas who would snatch her pages and eat them.

In the years since George Schaller and Dian Fossey began their work, many researchers have studied gorillas—not just the mountain gorillas but the other three subspecies as well. Thanks to all these scientists, we now know a lot about gorillas and how they live.

Family Ties

Just like people, gorillas' families are very important to them. Gorillas live in family groups, called troops, that travel through the forest together. Like any big family, they play, share food, and laugh with one another. Sometimes they get annoyed and quarrel or even scream in frustration. But in times of danger, they take care of each other.

Each family group is led by a male gorilla, usually an adult that's twelve years old or more, weighing about four hundred pounds. He's called a silverback because of the silvery gray fur that grows on the backs of older males. Each

Gorillas spend their days with family members close by.

day, the silverback decides where the group should go, when to stop and eat, and when it's time to bed down.

He mates with several females, and these mothers and their youngsters stay with him, often for many years. Young males, called black-backs, will sometimes be part of the group, but the silverback lets them know that he's in charge by growling and chasing the young ones when they get out of line. The younger males, as they grow older and stronger, watch for a chance to challenge the silverback. If they're strong enough, they might be able to defeat him in a fight and drive him away so that they can take over the leader role.

Gorilla troops usually have about a dozen members, although there might be fewer, and some troops can get as large as fifty or so. They move slowly through the forest, snacking on thistles, bamboo, and other leafy plants, and they love to crunch on wild celery. An adult gorilla will eat about forty pounds of plants a day, including lots of fruit, and some types of gorillas may eat a few insects as well. Even though they have huge fangs and powerful muscles, they don't hunt and kill other animals for food.

Unlike most rainforest mammals, which are active at night, gorillas are diurnal. This means they are awake and active during daylight hours and sleep at night. The troop only travels short distances on any given day, pausing often to rest and eat. During rest times, the elders snooze or forage for their favorite treats while the young ones chase each other, wrestle, and clamber about in the trees.

Silverbacks decide what the troop will do each day.

But gorillas aren't always peaceful. A celery-munching silverback will suddenly spring to his feet, beat his chest, and give off an earsplitting roar if danger looms—perhaps if a predator, like a leopard, gets too close. If two troops meet, the silverbacks may fight each other. They grasp each other with powerful arms, biting with their sharp teeth, often inflicting terrible wounds. Sometimes they fight to the death.

Growing Fears

As Dian Fossey observed the mountain gorillas year after year, she grew more and more impressed with how intelligent, loyal, and loving these huge animals could be. She was happiest when she was alone in the forest with her beloved gorillas, watching them grow up and getting to know their individual personalities. As she spent years observing and interacting with Digit's troop, she watched him grow to be a tall, strong adult.

But she also observed that the gorillas were increasingly facing risks from human activity. The area where the mountain gorillas lived was part of two national parks, set aside for the protection of wildlife. But the people who lived near the national parks were used to using the forest as a source of food and firewood, and even after the park was created, they would still go into the forest to hunt animals or chop down trees.

As the human population around the park grew, more and more farmers needed land to raise crops to feed their families. Almost half of the land that had been a protected park when George Schaller started his research was opened up to farming. The trees were cut or burned, and the land was cleared to make room for crops.

Farmers also wanted land to pasture their cows. Herds of hungry cattle would crash through the forest, trampling and eating plants that the gorillas needed for food. Trying to drive the cows away, Dian would furiously shout at them and fire a gun into the air, but they kept coming back. The gorillas' habitat was shrinking fast.

One of the major risks to the gorillas was the constant hunting of animals for food by illegal hunters, called poachers. They would set snares made of loops of wire, hidden so that the animals couldn't see the danger until they put a paw or a leg in the loop—then it would snap tight, trapping the animal. Even if the hunters were trying to catch other animals, like antelope, gorillas were often trapped in the snares. A wire loop could bind around a gorilla's ankle or wrist, leading to a painful infection and even death. Dian frantically tried to destroy as many snares as possible, but the poachers relentlessly continued hunting.

Tragedy in the Forest

In 1977, the troop that Dian's beloved Digit belonged to was threatened by a band of poachers. While the mothers and young fled to safety, Digit attacked the hunters fiercely. Though he had helped his family to escape, Digit himself wasn't as lucky. His body was found the next day by some of Dian's team members.

Dian was devasted by Digit's loss. And she was determined that Digit would not have died in vain. She dedicated the rest of her life to making the world aware of the threats that gorillas were facing.

She was featured in newspaper stories and magazine articles. Some were positive and some negative—many people didn't agree with her methods for stopping poachers, which were sometimes violent. She wrote a book called

Gorillas in the Mist, describing her life with the mountain gorillas. The book became a bestseller. She set up a charity called the Digit Fund, which raised money for anti-poaching patrols. On a visit to the United States, she went on television talk shows and was interviewed for magazines. She continued her education and became a college professor, teaching students about gorilla biology. Not long after Dian's death, a movie about her life with the gorillas was released, also called *Gorillas in the Mist*. Millions of people around the world began to realize how beautiful, fascinating, and important gorillas were—and how much trouble they were facing.

But was it too late to save the gorillas?

GORILLAS IN DANGER

How many gorillas remain in the wilds of the Congo Basin—and just how much trouble are they in? The answer is that no one knows for sure. But we know that there are so few gorillas that they are at serious risk of extinction.

Endangered species are animals that are in danger of disappearing from our planet. A group of scientists called the International Union for Conservation of Nature has a list called the IUCN Red List of Threatened Species™, which keeps track of all the endangered species in the world, including plants, animals, and even fungi. The animals are listed in seven categories: Least Concern and Near Threatened means the animals are mostly all right, but scientists are a little worried about them. Vulnerable, Endangered, and Critically Endangered mean that animals in those species are in trouble. Extinct in the Wild means the animals still exist in zoos, so there is at least the hope of someday bringing them back to their homes. Extinct is the last category, and that means that the animals are gone from the world, never to return.

Shrinking Habitat

Dian Fossey feared for the future of her beloved gorillas when she saw their forest habitat being replaced by farms, cattle range, and houses.

Habitat loss is a problem for almost all endangered species. If the animal has a wide range, with populations spread far apart over many different areas, there's a better chance the species will survive. But gorillas live in one place and one place only—and their rainforest habitat is getting smaller.

Gorillas' rainforest home is getting smaller every year.

Gorilla Habitats

The land around the national parks is home to some of the most densely populated areas in the world. Rwanda, for example, is a small country, with a landmass about the size of the state of Massachusetts but with twice as many people living in it. For thousands of years, the Congo Basin has provided food, shelter, and more to people and animals alike. But as the population grows, more and more people are using up resources that animals have relied upon in the past.

And on top of the needs of people who compete with the gorillas for habitat, millions of acres of forest are destroyed every year to open up land for farming—not only for growing crops to feed hungry people but to grow nonessential items like coffee or chocolate. Most of the world's chocolate and a lot of its coffee comes from equatorial Africa—the same region where most of the world's gorillas live. These crops can only be grown in warm, moist climates, and the area around the equator has the exact kind of environment they need. These products are mostly sold by big corporations for huge profits in the US and other countries.

Also, millions of acres of rainforest are destroyed to make room for a product called palm oil. This is an oil made from the fruit of oil palm trees, and it's used in an endless variety of products. The thick, smooth oil helps potato chips stay crispy, ice cream taste creamy, and cookies feel chewy. It can even make soap and shampoo more bubbly. About half of the packaged products for sale in any supermarket are likely to contain palm oil: edible items like cereal, margarine, and pet food, as well as other things like toothpaste and lipstick. It's also commonly used in cheap fast foods like hamburgers, pizza, and doughnuts.

Some African countries have lost almost all of their rainforest, largely because of intensive farming. The last few of the most critically endangered gorillas, the Cross River gorillas, are especially threatened by pressure to turn the last bits of Nigerian rainforest into farms.

Rainforests are also cut down by big logging companies. Giant trees are turned into paper towels, chairs, tables, or planks for floors. A family looking for firewood might cut down a few trees but would leave much of the undergrowth in place. But a big logging company uses heavy equipment to clear-cut an enormous swath of forest. Clear-cutting means chain-sawing or bulldozing every single tree, leaving nothing but bare earth that quickly washes away in heavy rains.

As remote areas of the forest are cut, truckers need roads to transport heavy loads of logs. New roads make it easier for poachers to reach distant areas of the forest. As their habitat is divided into smaller and smaller pieces, gorillas have fewer areas to shelter in.

Poaching

For many years, relentless poaching has been one of the greatest threats to gorillas. *Bushmeat* is the term used for food that comes from wild animals, including gorillas. Poachers sell low-cost bushmeat to people who need to feed their hungry families. Gorillas are also sometimes hunted so that their meat can be sold to high-end restaurants for wealthy customers who prize ape meat as a delicacy.

Gorilla body parts are also highly valued in some African communities for use as medicine, even though they have no medical value at all. In some traditional cultures, ape body parts are used for the making of charms that are believed to provide protection from evil spirits, bad luck, or witchcraft. Killing just one gorilla provides hundreds of pounds of meat as well as valuable body parts to sell. That means a big financial profit for a poacher, so even though gorilla hunting is against the law, poachers continue to hunt and kill them anyway.

Gorillas have such closely knit families that what happens to one gorilla affects the others deeply. Young males sometimes will act as sentries to warn the troop of danger. Older females help raise and guard the youngsters.

Grown-ups teach young gorillas which plants are best to eat and how to find them. And the silverback defends the whole troop and also uses his years of experience to guide them to good feeding spots or keep them out of trouble. Even the loss of one or two gorillas in a troop

Baby gorillas need their families around them in order to survive.

can make it much harder for the other family members to survive.

Like humans, gorillas reproduce slowly. Unlike, say, rabbits that can have forty or more babies in a single year, a mother gorilla has one baby at a time—twins are rare. She tends to her baby carefully for many months and might not have another for five years or so. With so many gorillas being killed, it will take many decades for them to rebuild their populations.

The Tragedy of War

When war ravages a nation, it's not just people who suffer—wildlife does, too. Civil wars and conflicts in Rwanda and the DRC have killed millions of people and forced others to flee from their homes. This violence has been a tragedy for gorillas as well as for people.

In the violence and chaos of war, national park boundaries are ignored as starving people use wildlife for food and cut trees for firewood to keep warm. In times of war, there's no money to pay park rangers or police. Poachers and traders who deal in illegal products are almost never arrested. Universities are closed, and wildlife research comes to a halt. So does wildlife protection sometimes. Even after the war is over, it can take many years for life to begin to return to normal.

Gorillas and the people who are trying to help them are impacted by all of this. Both George Schaller and Dian Fossey were forced to flee their research stations when violence threatened, and researchers, guides, and park rangers can still find themselves in dangerous situations today.

Health Matters

Sadly, one way in which gorillas and humans are very similar is that they can get many of the same diseases and have many of the same health problems. Just like people, gorillas in zoos sometimes eat too much sugar and don't get enough exercise. This can lead to tooth decay, diabetes, and heart disease. In the rainforest, gorillas tend to be much healthier, as they constantly rove through the forest and eat wild plants. But their wild home is increasingly being visited by their human neighbors.

Only half a century ago, humans and gorillas rarely laid eyes on each other. Now many gorilla populations are surrounded by people. Poachers, loggers, and farmers can all spread human diseases to gorillas. Even people who love gorillas, like researchers, photographers, or tourists, can spread germs. Just as with people, one sneeze can infect others. Gorillas get runny noses, coughs, and fevers like humans do. But even a mild cold that wouldn't kill a human can be deadly to gorillas. Tourists who visit gorilla troops to see and photograph them have to agree never to try to touch gorillas or approach them too closely. Visitors to gorilla territory are asked to wear masks and stay at least twenty feet away from the animals.

A terrible disease called Ebola Virus Disease can sicken and kill both gorillas and humans. In 1995, 90 percent of the gorillas in Minkébé National Park in Gabon died from Ebola.

If you've ever visited gorillas in a zoo, you probably watched them through a thick window of unbreakable glass. That's to keep the gorillas warm and sheltered from cold drafts but also to protect them from human germs. Zookeepers work hard to keep the gorillas active and healthy. Zoo gorillas get their annual flu shots and are also vaccinated against measles. During the coronavirus pandemic, gorillas were at risk of getting COVID-19 just as humans were, and

Who's watching who?

some even tested positive. In many zoos in the United States and around the world, gorillas were given the COVID-19 vaccine to protect them against the disease.

Time to Get Busy

Gorillas face so many threats and challenges to their survival that it can seem like the problems are impossible to solve. How can anyone prevent wars in distant countries or stop deadly diseases? How can we save the rainforest from being cut down or keep animals safe from poachers' snares? How can we protect these animals that live so far away from most of us?

If you're anxious about gorillas and want to help them, you're not alone. Like Dian Fossey, many people love gorillas and are angry about what's happening to them. And these people, all over the world, are turning their love and their anger into powerful action to help gorillas survive.

One of the first steps to saving an endangered species is to let people know about these magnificent animals and find a way to get them excited to learn more. And it turns out that one of the best ways to get the world interested in gorillas was to let a very remarkable gorilla speak for herself!

4

GIVING GORILLAS A HELPING HAND

Robin reached out and tickled Koko under the arm. Koko chuckled and tickled him back. Then they tickled each other, both rolling on the ground and laughing out loud. Still giggling, they shared a warm, loving hug. Robin was a human being. Koko was a gorilla.

Koko was born in the San Francisco Zoo in 1971, but when she was just a baby, she became very sick. Francine Patterson (often called Penny) was a wildlife researcher who helped nurse Koko back to health. She then began to work with the little gorilla, trying to learn more about how gorillas communicate. Gorillas use sounds to "talk" to each other, but they don't have the same muscles around their lips and tongues that humans do, so they can't speak words aloud. Penny got the idea of using American Sign Language—a language that relies on hand motions instead of sounds, and is used by people who are deaf or hard of hearing.

She worked with Koko for years and taught her more than a thousand signs. Koko's vocabulary wasn't just words for simple things like *banana* or *toy*. She used signs to share her feelings, with words like *happy*, *sad*, *mad*, *hurry*, *anxious*, and *sorry*. When Koko seemed lonely, she was given a kitten as a pet to keep her company. The plump little kitten didn't have a tail, and Koko named her All Ball. The huge gorilla cradled the tiny kitten tenderly. She crossed her arms across her chest to sign *love*.

Penny wrote a book about Koko and All Ball called *Koko's Kitten*. Kids all over the world read it and fell in love with Koko and her beloved pet. Koko was on the cover of magazines and was visited by television and movie stars like Mister Rogers and comedian Robin Williams. She and Robin had a wonderful time together—she tried on his glasses, played tag with him, and enjoyed a tickle fight.

Communicating with Koko helped people understand how gorillas think, what they need, and what makes them happy. This has helped zookeepers figure out how to better care for gorillas that are kept in zoos. And getting to know Koko made people around the world become interested in these amazing animals. Koko helped us realize that gorillas are not that different from us, and that gorillas in the wild desperately need our help.

Keeping an Eye on Gorillas

Many scientists and not-for-profit organizations are working with the governments of African countries to find ways to protect gorillas. One of the first steps in protecting any endangered species is to learn as much as possible about what that animal needs to survive—what kinds of foods it depends on, where the mothers have their babies, what diseases it suffers from, what dangers it faces. But if you want to study wild gorillas, first you have to find them.

Ossolo Dacko is a professional tracker who

works at the Dzanga-Sangha Protected Area, which is home to Western lowland gorillas in the Central African Republic. His job is to locate the gorillas that roam the forest so that teams of researchers can observe them. The gorillas move to new feeding spots every day, but Ossolo knows the clues to look for as he hikes through the thick, humid rainforest. Here's a bamboo plant, chewed and splintered. Here's a knuckle print in the mud. Here's an overturned log, or a nest of broken branches and soft grass. A good clue is a pile of gorilla scat (also known as poop). Examining the scat can tell trackers like Ossolo a lot of things—what the gorilla has been eating, how healthy it is, and even how long it's been since the animal was there. If the poop is still warm, the gorilla isn't far away!

Ossolo is just one of many people who

work as wildlife trackers, park rangers, and researchers in the nations of Africa. Most of the gorilla troops that live in national parks and nature preserves are closely watched and guarded. These troops are habituated to humans, which means they are so used to people observing them at close range that they go about their normal activities without being overly stressed by their human visitors. Members of a troop might play with other gorillas, groom and hug each other, forage for food, climb trees, or even doze off while tourists are watching and taking photographs. Habituation lets researchers study the gorillas' behaviors and also keep a sharp eye on their health.

In addition to helping scientists find gorillas, trackers like Ossolo also lead groups of tourists along the forest trails so that they can see

It's a thrill to glimpse a gorilla in the wild.

the animals. Tens of thousands of people come every year to have the thrill of a lifetime by getting close to a wild gorilla.

Tourism brings many millions of dollars to the countries where gorillas live. Gorilla watchers stay in hotels, eat in restaurants, and shop in stores. That means jobs for people who work in those places, as well as jobs for trackers, guides, veterinarians, and anti-poacher guards.

Gorilla Doctors

When a species that's endangered has only a few individuals left, every life counts. And sometimes when a gorilla is in trouble, a timely doctor's visit can make all the difference. In some of the parks and preserves where gorillas live, veterinarians make "house calls" to the forest to care for sick or injured gorillas.

A gorilla doctor treats their patient very much like a human doctor treats you. The doctor might listen to the gorilla's heart and lungs with a stethoscope, take the patient's temperature, or prescribe antibiotics to prevent or treat infection. A gorilla vet might set a broken limb, take a blood sample, or stitch up a wound.

One problem that wildlife veterinarians often face is deciding when it's appropriate to try to help the animals. Being caught and held down while a vet takes care of a wound can be stressful for the gorilla. The rest of the gorillas in the troop can also become very upset while their family member is being tended to. Sometimes gorillas are shot with a dart gun containing a dose of medicine so that the vet never needs to touch the animal. Sometimes the gorilla patient is darted with a drug to make them sleepy and relaxed while they're being helped. But these tranquilizers can be harmful to the gorilla if the dose isn't just right.

If the problem is something caused in the usual course of a gorilla's life—a bite from another gorilla, a fall from a tree—the vet may decide to let nature take its course. But if the injury or illness is caused by humans—a bad cold picked up from a tourist or an infection from a poacher's snare—the doctors will usually act to help the gorilla.

Good News

Not long ago, the future of mountain gorillas looked bleak. In 1980, in spite of the work of Dian Fossey and other conservationists, there were only about 250 of the animals left in the wild, and none were being kept in zoos anywhere in the world. Wildlife biologists feared that the whole subspecies was doomed, headed for certain extinction in just a short time. But over the years, the intense efforts by many people to save these magnificent creatures have begun to pay off.

Every day, brave guards and park rangers

risk their lives to scare away armed poachers and remove deadly snares from the forest. Gorilla doctors use their skills and the techniques of modern medicine to keep gorillas healthy. And the publicity that mountain gorillas received from Dian Fossey's bestselling book and the movie that was made from it has

Much of the money Dian Fossey raised went to form patrols of anti-poacher guards to protect the gorillas.

helped bring in huge contributions of money to fund rescue and protection efforts.

In 2018 it was announced that, unlike all other gorilla subspecies, mountain gorillas are no longer Critically Endangered. Their population is almost four times what it was when Dian Fossey began to work with them. Although they're still on the Red List as Endangered, there is hope that mountain gorilla populations will keep that upward trend.

There's Still a Lot of Work Ahead

But what about the gorillas that live far away from guards and veterinarians? Most gorillas don't live in parks and preserves. Some gorillas live in areas that are surrounded by large human populations and are sometimes injured when crossing roads or venturing into crop fields or gardens. Others are found in areas that are too remote, or too dangerous, for tourists, scientists, and doctors to venture. The other three subspecies of gorillas have not gotten the attention and publicity that have helped mountain gorillas come back from the verge of extinction.

In addition to guarding the gorillas in parks, we need to find ways to help the gorillas that live outside their borders. And that means protecting the habitat they need to survive.

The Congo rainforest is the home of wild animals, but it's also been a source of human food and fuel for thousands of years. Wildlife and humans both need the forest. And if a forest is taken care of in a way that is sustainable, it can meet the needs of both people and wildlife.

To do something sustainably means that

we can use a resource without destroying it. Logging and farming are two of the greatest threats to the rainforest, but both of these activities can be done in ways that are more sustainable.

Sustainable forestry means more than just planting new trees to replace the ones that have been cut down. It means figuring out which kinds of trees are most needed by animals and leaving some trees standing to provide seeds for the future. It's important to find ways to remove logs from the forest carefully, without damaging the soil or creating wide roadways that cause erosion, where the soil gets swept away so new trees can't grow. Wood that is harvested sustainably can provide profitable jobs for the people who have always depended on the forest—and keep the forest healthy for future generations of both wildlife and humans.

Farming can also be done in a more sustainable way. For example, it turns out that both coffee and chocolate can grow well even under the shade of taller trees. Some people even think that shade-grown chocolate tastes better! Leaving tall trees standing, especially fruit trees, means a farm can feed and shelter wildlife while the farmer is able to grow a crop and sell it. It's possible to grow crops like palm oil, coffee, or chocolate in a way that won't destroy the forest. And there are ways to make products like ice cream, toothpaste, margarine, and others using different ingredients instead of palm oil.

Lemonade for Gorillas

The Congo rainforest is very far from where most of us live. But one gorilla lover has found a way to help gorillas from thousands of miles away.

Addy Barrett was only in first grade when she read a book about mountain gorillas. "I really fell in love with how smart they are and how they relate to us," she remembers. When she visited the National Zoo in Washington, D.C., she spent hours watching Moke, a playful young gorilla. But when she discovered that her favorite animals were endangered, she decided to take action. "I learned they were being poached and killed," she said. "I needed to do something!"

Addy started small, with a sidewalk lemonade stand that raised a few dollars. Then she began to think bigger. She organized bake sales, craft fairs, and raffles, donating all the money to not-for-profit organizations that help gorillas. When she turned twelve, Addy started a website she called Gorilla Heroes. Her Gorilla Gala fundraising events are sometimes sponsored by big corporations like Gorilla Glue.

One of Addy's events raised money to buy toys for gorillas in the National Zoo. Toys for gorillas? Captive animals can suffer from boredom in the enclosed space of a zoo, and challenging toys and puzzles can keep them busy and interested. One of the most popular gorilla toys is a length of colorful knotted ropes that the agile fingers of the big apes can twist, tug, and manipulate. But most of the money Addy has raised—more than fifteen thousand dollars!—goes directly to the Dian Fossey Gorilla Fund (which used to be called the Digit Fund) and other wildlife organizations that work to help gorillas in their rainforest home.

Why Save the Gorillas?

Some people might ask: Why bother saving gorillas at all? Does it really matter to our daily lives if gorillas are endangered or not? But by working to save gorilla habitat, we're also working to help ourselves.

Rainforests grow far away from where most of us live. But rainforests affect you with every breath you take. The billions of trees in the rainforest make food for themselves out of water, air, and sunlight in a process called photosynthesis. And fortunately for us humans, during photosynthesis plants give off oxygen, which we can't live without.

Trees also transpire, which means that they give off water into the air. This water vapor forms into clouds that then travel all over the world. Rain clouds that are created above the

Congo Basin may bring rainfall many thousands of miles away—maybe to your neighborhood! Deforestation, or destruction of forests, means less water is released into the atmosphere. This means less rainfall and increasing droughts all over the world.

One of the biggest threats to our planet is climate change, which is caused by gases called greenhouse gases that trap the sun's heat and keep it close to the earth. Carbon dioxide (CO_2) is one of the main pollutants that cause climate change. Human activities, like driving cars and burning oil and coal in power plants, pump billions of tons of CO_2 into the air.

But again, it's trees to the rescue! Another good thing that happens during photosynthesis is that CO_2 is removed from the atmosphere. As they're making food, rainforest trees absorb huge amounts of carbon dioxide from the atmosphere. So rainforests can help lessen the disastrous effects of climate change, like extreme and frequent droughts, floods, and storms. Gorillas probably don't realize that with every seed-filled poop, they're planting trees that fight climate change!

Look into a Gorilla's Eyes

With so many people working to help them, there's hope that gorillas will always roam their green rainforest, laughing, playing, loving, and protecting their families. Gorillas are part of our world—our close relatives, who have much to teach us. "No one who looks into a gorilla's eyes—intelligent, gentle, vulnerable—can remain unchanged," George Schaller wrote. "We know that the gorilla still lives within us."

The gorillas' world is changing, and so is ours. The most important way in which gorillas and humans are alike is that we all need clean air to breathe, fresh water to drink, and a healthy planet to live on. We're all in this together.

When we look into a gorilla's eyes, we see ourselves.

BIG SHAGGY FACTS ABOUT GORILLAS

1. Each gorilla has a "noseprint." This is a series of wrinkles above the nostrils that's a little different from all other gorillas, just like human fingerprints. Researchers use photos or sketches of noseprints to identify individual gorillas.

2. Gorillas are highly intelligent animals. They know how to use sticks as tools for gathering fruit. In the wild, they've even used sticks to measure water depth.

3. How strong are gorillas? Very strong! Silverbacks have been known to escape

from cages in zoos by bending iron bars.

4. Gorillas have a bite force of about 1,300 pounds per square inch. A human's bite force is about seventy pounds per square inch. A gorilla can bite twice as hard as a lion!

5. Gorillas can live a long time. Fatou, a gorilla in the Berlin Zoo, celebrated her sixty-fifth birthday in April 2022! In the wild, their life span is more likely to be about thirty-five years.

6. Gorillas' arms are longer than their legs. They can walk upright like humans but usually only for short periods of time.

7. Unlike most apes and monkeys, gorillas don't spend much time in trees. Adults will climb them to gather fruit and youngsters will scramble about the

branches while playing. Some gorillas will even build their sleeping nests in trees. But gorillas spend most of their time on the ground.

8. An adult gorilla eats about forty pounds of vegetation a day. That's about ten times as much as an adult human eats!

9. Gorilla hands are a lot like human hands, covered with bare skin and not fur. With agile fingers and thumbs, gorillas can easily pick up small objects.

10. When baby gorillas are newborns, they're even tinier than most human infants, weighing only about four or five pounds. Gorilla mothers nurse their babies for several years.

11. While humans might have several dif-

ferent eye colors, all gorillas have dark brown eyes.

12. Like humans, gorillas do not swim naturally. In search of food, they will sometimes wade through chest-deep water, standing upright. Gorillas have occasionally been observed playing in shallow water.

HOW YOU CAN HELP SAVE THE GORILLAS

You may love gorillas, but chances are you won't be seeing one in your neighborhood anytime soon. So you might not think that things you do could have any effect on creatures that live so far away. But it turns out that you can help gorillas in a lot of ways.

1. Shop for gorillas! Learn more about products, like chocolate, that can be grown in a way that doesn't destroy the rainforest. Read labels carefully, and be wary of ingredients, especially palm

oil, that are grown in ways that damage wildlife habitats. An organization called Roundtable on Sustainable Palm Oil (RSPO) certifies farms that grow sustainable palm oil so that companies can label their products as rainforest-friendly.

2. Learn how to buy rainforest-friendly products with Rainforest Alliance's Follow the Frog campaign. This organization gives a seal of approval to products that are produced sustainably. Look for products labeled with a picture of a rainforest tree frog. You can find out more at Rainforest-Alliance.org.

3. Encourage your family to buy only sustainable wood. Just as when you shop in grocery stores, read labels! If your family is buying building materials or

furniture, try to find out if wood products have been harvested sustainably.

4. Spread the word about gorillas. Host a World Gorilla Day event at your school, do a science fair project, or consider working with an adult to use social media to let people know about the challenges gorillas face. Perhaps you could research an individual gorilla you'd like to know more about, like Digit or Koko. Several organizations have biographies of gorillas on their websites, including the Dian Fossey Gorilla Fund, Gorilla Doctors, and Kids4Koko (see below).

5. Celebrate World Gorilla Day on September 24 each year.

6. Give a gorilla a birthday present! Use your special day or other holidays to ask

friends and family to donate to organizations that are fighting to protect wildlife, including:

- Dian Fossey Gorilla Fund International (GorillaFund.org)
- Gorilla Doctors (GorillaDoctors.org)
- The Gorilla Foundation (which has information about Koko) (Koko.org)

7. Adopt a gorilla. Some organizations, including the World Wildlife Fund and the Dian Fossey Gorilla Fund, offer adoption programs. You or your class could symbolically adopt an animal and receive updates on its life.

8. Learn to talk like a gorilla! Check out Koko .org/Kids4Koko. You can watch videos of Koko and her friends signing, and learn some of the sign language Koko used.

9. Recycle your phone! Many of the metals that cell phones and other electronics are made of are mined from gorilla habitats. By recycling your phone, and encouraging others to do the same, you help preserve habitats.

10. Write to your representatives in government and urge them to take action to protect gorillas. Generally, their contact information is easily available on the internet. You can go to House.gov to find out who your representative is.

11. VOTE! Support political candidates who support protecting the environment. Register to vote as soon as you can, and encourage everyone you know to vote with the environment in mind.

ACKNOWLEDGMENTS

Thanks to all the people, past and present, who have done so much to save the gorillas and their rainforest home!

REFERENCES

Cross River Gorilla Programme. "What We Do: Habitat Loss." Cross River Gorilla Conservation. African Conservation Foundation and Environment & Rural Development Foundation. https://crossrivergorilla.org/habitat-loss.

Daly, Natasha. "First Great Apes at U.S. Zoo Receive COVID-19 Vaccine." Animals. *National Geographic*, March 3, 2021. https://www.nationalgeographic.com/animals/article/first-great-apes-at-us-zoo-receive-coronavirus-vaccine-made-for-animals.

Elasfar, Dara. "A Passion to Save Gorillas Makes One 11-Year-Old a 'Hero.'" *The Washington Post*, September 23, 2019. https://www.washingtonpost

.com/lifestyle/kidspost/11-year-old-aims-to-save
-gorillas-and-one-day-visit-them/2019/09/23
/de7abfd8-d291-11e9-9610-fb56c5522e1c_story
.html.

Fauna & Flora International. "Explore: Species:
Grauer's Gorilla." Fauna & Flora International.
https://www.fauna-flora.org/species/grauers
-gorilla.

Fossey, Dian. *Gorillas in the Mist*. Boston, MA:
Houghton Mifflin, 1983.

Gorilla Doctors. "Saving Lives: Disease and Trauma in
Gorillas." https://www.gorilladoctors.org/saving
-lives/gorilla-health-threats/infectious-disease.

Gorilla Heroes. Accessed December 4, 2021.
https://1532232.wixsite.com/gorillahero
?msclkid=f9cf466dbd8d11ec9a2aa207982f4c74.

Isaacson, Andy. "The First Rule of Gorilla
Tracking? Listen Well." World Wildlife Fund,
May 5, 2020. https://www.worldwildlife.org
/stories/the-first-rule-of-gorilla-tracking-listen-well.

Mowat, Farley. *Woman in the Mists: The Story of Dian Fossey and the Mountain Gorillas of Africa*. New York, NY: Warner Books, 1987.

Patterson, Francine, and Eugene Linden. *The Education of Koko*. New York, NY: Holt, Rinehart, and Winston, 1981.

Petre, Charles-Albert, Nikki Tag, Barbara Haurez, Roseline Beudels-Jamar, Marie-Claude Huynen, and Jean-Louis Doucet. "Role of the Western Gorilla (*Gorilla gorilla gorilla*) in Seed Dispersal in Tropical Forests and Implications of Its Decline." *Biotechnology, Agronomy, Society and Environment* 17, no. 3 (May 2013): 517–526. https://popups .uliege.be/1780-4507/index.php?id=10293.

Rainforest Alliance. "Insights: What is Sustainable Agriculture?" Rainforest Alliance. Last modified October 7, 2019. https://www.rainforest-alliance .org/insights/what-is-sustainable-agriculture.

Russon, Anne E., and Janette Wallis, eds. *Primate Tourism: A Tool for Conservation?* Cambridge, UK: Cambridge University Press, 2014.

Schaller, George B. "Gentle Gorillas, Turbulent Times." *National Geographic* 188, no. 4 (October 1995): 65–68.

Schaller, George B. *The Mountain Gorilla: Ecology and Behavior*. Chicago, IL: University of Chicago Press, 2000.

Schaller, George B. *The Year of the Gorilla*. Chicago, IL: University of Chicago Press, 1964.

Silvey, Anita. *Unforgotten: The Wild Life of Dian Fossey and Her Relentless Quest to Save Mountain Gorillas*. Washington, D.C.: National Geographic Society, 2021.

Smithsonian's National Zoo & Conservation Biology Institute. "Animals: Western Lowland Gorilla." Smithsonian's National Zoo & Conservation Biology Institute. https://nationalzoo.si.edu/animals/western-lowland-gorilla.

Wildlife Conservation Society. "Wildlife: Gorillas." Wildlife Conservation Society. https://www.wcs.org/our-work/species/gorillas.

ANITA SANCHEZ is especially fascinated by plants and animals that no one loves and by the unusual, often ignored wild places of the world. Her award-winning books sing the praises of the unappreciated: dandelions, poison ivy, tarantulas, mud puddles. Her goal is to make young readers excited about science and nature. Many years of fieldwork and teaching outdoor classes have given her firsthand experience in introducing students to the wonders of the natural world.

Photo by George Steele

You can visit Anita Sanchez online at
AnitaSanchez.com
and follow her on Twitter
@ASanchezAuthor

CHELSEA CLINTON is the author of the #1 *New York Times* bestseller *She Persisted: 13 American Women Who Changed the World*; *She Persisted Around the World: 13 Women Who Changed History*; *She Persisted in Sports: American Olympians Who Changed the Game*; *Don't Let Them Disappear: 12 Endangered Species Across the Globe*; *It's Your World: Get Informed, Get Inspired & Get Going!*; *Start Now!: You Can Make a Difference*; with Hillary Clinton, *Grandma's Gardens* and *The Book of Gutsy Women: Favorite Stories of Courage and Resilience*; and, with Devi Sridhar, *Governing Global Health: Who Runs the World and Why?* She is also the Vice Chair of the Clinton Foundation, where she works on many initiatives, including those that help empower the next generation of leaders. She lives in New York City with her husband, Marc, their children and their dog, Soren.

Photo courtesy of the author

You can follow Chelsea Clinton on Twitter
@ChelseaClinton
or on Facebook at
Facebook.com/ChelseaClinton

DON'T MISS MORE BOOKS IN THE

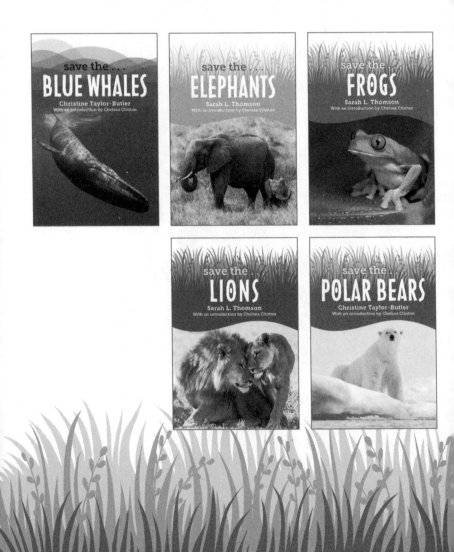

save the... SERIES!